# Handmade Scandinavian
# CHRISTMAS

HEGE BARNHOLT

D&C
David and Charles

A DAVID & CHARLES BOOK
© Cappelen Damm AS 2012

Originally published in Norway as Julens Skattkammer

First published in the UK and USA in 2013 by F&W Media International, Ltd

David & Charles is an imprint of F&W Media International, Ltd
Brunel House, Forde Close, Newton Abbot, TQ12 4PU, UK

F&W Media International, Ltd is a subsidiary of F+W Media, Inc
10151 Carver Road, Suite #200, Blue Ash, OH 45242, USA

A catalogue record for this book is available from the British Library.

ISBN-13: 978-1-4463-0361-0 hardback
ISBN-10: 1-4463-0361-6 hardback

ISBN-13: 978-1-4463-0362-7 paperback
ISBN-10: 1-4463-0362-4 paperback

Printed in China by RR Donnelley for:
F&W Media International, Ltd
Brunel House, Forde Close, Newton Abbot, TQ12 4PU, UK

10 9 8 7 6 5 4 3 2 1

Photographer: Bjørn Johan Stenersen
Stylist: Hege Barnholt
Book design: Hanne Marie Kjus

F+W Media publishes high quality books on a wide range of subjects.
For more great book ideas visit: www.stitchcraftcreate.co.uk

# CONTENTS

# Christmas is all about expectation, excitement, joy, good feeling, and of course, tradition.

Ever since I was a child, I've started the Christmas preparations in October. When the forest becomes a colourful fairy tale and the first frost makes the ground crisp, I am filled with excitement and anticipation about the wonderful festive season.

I still feel that same excitement now. It is a privilege to be able to start Christmas in the forest; collecting twigs and cones, carefully placing colourful leaves in my basket and cutting out pieces of moss. Now I can start planning how I want to shape my own Christmas, beginning with making small presents for the people that I care about. I've even managed to convince my husband to make me an advent calendar! It was difficult, but now I can see him carefully hiding away little things, starting in November.

You can therefore imagine my excitement when I was presented with the opportunity to write a Christmas book. A book about everything I love: can it get any better?

I hope this book will inspire you and your family, both young and old, to create your own Christmas traditions. Gather your family for some Christmas crafting and spread joy and excitement in the lead-up to Christmas. Let the children create their own treasure chest with presents and decorations that they have made themselves.

Have fun creating a wealth of happy memories and making your own festive family traditions to treasure in years to come.

*Hege Barnholt*

# Preparing for
# Christmas

Get your boots on and warm clothes out and pour some hot soup from a Thermos. A walk in the autumn forest is an exploration of exciting colours and shapes. A hunt for pretty leaves, hips, cones, moss and crooked branches – everything can be used for something. It is a truly enjoyable experience and the perfect way to start your Christmas preparations.

# JUNIPER CANDLE WREATH

This atmospheric candle wreath, made using juniper twigs, instantly evokes happy, festive memories.

**You will need:**

- Juniper twigs
- Wooden beads, 2.5cm (1in)
- Candle holders
- Red candles
- Red and white string
- Wire (or iron wreath)
- Pincers

**THIS IS WHAT YOU DO:**

- Wind the wire in a circle.
- Repeat the circle multiple times until the wreath is stable. Alternatively, you can use a small iron wreath.
- Make small bouquets of juniper.
- Place the bouquets on the wreath so they overlap each other.
- Attach the bouquets with winding wire.
- Tie red and white string in four different places on the wreath for hanging.
- Thread four wooden beads on each string.
- Tie the four threads together and make a loop for hanging at the top.
- Clip on four candle holders.
- Place candles in the holders.

Follow these simple steps and use beautiful, rustic materials to quickly create a romantic, festive atmosphere on your table.

Some days deserve both napkin rings and place cards! Your guests will really appreciate their personal welcome at dinner (and the children can be kept busy making these while you set the table).

# ALDER CONE NAPKIN RING

**You will need:**

- Cones from an alder
- Cardboard letters
- Labels
- Thick, red cotton thread
- Wax thread

**THIS IS WHAT YOU DO:**

- Wind the wax thread once around the alder cone.
- Repeat with additional alder cones, placing them beside each other until you have created a large enough ring to wrap around the napkin.
- Glue the guest's first initial onto the label.
- Tie the label to the napkin ring using the thick, red cotton thread.

# ROWAN-BERRY CANDLE JAR

**You will need:**

- Pine cones
- Rowan-berries
- Hazel leaves
- Small juniper branches
- Yellow acrylic paint
- Hemp rope
- Jars
- Tealight candles
- Glue gun

**THIS IS WHAT YOU DO:**

- Paint the leaves on both sides using yellow acrylic paint then set them aside to dry.
- Make a bundle of pine cones, rowan-berries, hazel leaves and juniper branches. (A glue gun can be helpful.)
- Attach the bundles around each jar using hemp rope.
- Use only tealight candles inside the jars.

# SPRUCE CONE VASE

You don't need to venture far into the woods to find
the materials to make this stunning cone vase.

**You will need:**

- Spruce cones
- Test tubes
- Wire
- Hemp rope
- Glue gun
  (optional)

**THIS IS WHAT YOU DO:**

- Pick out the prettiest four cones.
- Bundle them together, placing a test tube in the centre.
- Wind wire around the bundle a couple of times.
  Alternatively, attach the test tube and cones with glue
  to make the vase more stable.
- Tie hemp rope around the vase to decorate.

# LARCH GARLAND

Hang this beautiful garland on a mirror, a light coloured wall, or simply place it on a serving dish.

**You will need:**

- Bark hearts from Panduro (or cut them out yourself from the bark of a birch tree)
- Cones from a larch tree
- Wooden beads
- Waxed thread
- Hole punch plier

**THIS IS WHAT YOU DO:**

- Tie a loop in one end of the thread.
- Make a hole in the hearts with the hole punch plier.
- Tie the cones together in pairs using the waxed thread.
- Attach the heart to the thread.
- Repeat using a different number of cones between the hearts.
- Finish up by tying a wooden bead at the end of the thread to add weight to the garland.

# HANDSEWN BRANCH DECORATIONS

These stitch-embellished, hanging decorations are a playful and decorative way to dress your Christmas tree. Hung up, they create a stylish contrast to the traditional tree.

## You will need:

- One thick branch
- Embroidery yarn in different colours
- Sewing needle
- Wax thread for hanging
- Saw
- Drill

### THIS IS WHAT YOU DO:

- Saw thin slices of a thick branch.
- Sketch, e.g. a star or a heart, with a pencil.
- Drill thin holes along the lines and a hole at the top for hanging.
- Backstitch in the holes with embroidery yarn.
- Use wax thread for hanging in the top.

# WOODEN TREE DECORATIONS

It's unbelievable what you can create from a thick branch or a log of wood!

## You will need:

- Thick branch or log of wood
- Red and white ribbon
- Compass saw
- Knife or razor
- Drill

### THIS IS WHAT YOU DO:

- Take a level log with thick and rugged bark, maybe even with some moss.
- Level out the backside so that it is as even as possible using a knife or razor.
- Sketch out your desired shape on your log (see Templates).
- Cut out the figure using a compass saw. (NB: you should have some experience with a compass saw to try this one.)
- Drill a hole in the top for hanging.

# MOSS BALLS

Moss, or the evergreen forest floor, creates a nice atmosphere on dark nights.

**You will need:**

- Moss
- Oasis
- Cones from alder or sticks
- Wire
- Coarse twine
- Pincers

**THIS IS WHAT YOU DO:**

- Use ball-shaped oasis or cut out balls from an oasis block.
- Soak the oasis in water to keep the moss green for longer.
- Place flakes of moss around each oasis ball.
- Wind wire around the ball to attach the moss.
- Tie the coarse twine around the ball three times and finish off with a knot for hanging.
- Attach sticks or alder cones for decoration.

# STICK CHRISTMAS TREES

Use these quirky Christmas trees to beautifully decorate the table, or perhaps use them as place cards for Christmas dinner.

**You will need:**

- One thick branch
- Small sticks
- Brown paper
- Glue
- Saw
- Drill

**THIS IS WHAT YOU DO:**

- Saw thin slices of a thick branch.
- Drill a small hole in the middle of the slice.
- Place the stick into the hole
- Sketch two stars from a small cookie cutter, or using the template provided (see Templates), onto the brown paper.
- Glue the brown paper stars together and secure them to the top of each stick.

Hearts and stars are beautiful by themselves, but you can add something special by positioning a plywood bird in the centre.

# BIRCH HEART

Did the snow fall 'before you knew it'?
Don't worry!

**You will need:**

- A few thin and flexible birch branches
- A small fir twig
- Wire
- Pincers

**THIS IS WHAT YOU DO:**

- Cut the birch branches in pieces measuring about
  1m (1yd) in length.
- Make the branches more flexible by bending
  them carefully.
- Tie the branches together with wire.
- Split the bundle evenly into two and connect the ends
  together using wire.
- Pull the top down – and shape the branches into a heart.
- Wind with wire to secure the heart shape.
- Attach a small fir branch twig with wire to embellish.

# GREEN WREATH

It is so simple and so natural.

**You will need:**

- Iron wreath
- Green flat moss
- Cowberry bush
- Pine cones
- Wire
- Pincers

**THIS IS WHAT YOU DO:**

- Squeeze the moss around the wreath.
- Put some cowberry bush over the moss.
- Wind the wire around the moss and cowberry bush.
- Continue until you have covered the entire heart.
- Attach two pine cones in the middle of the heart shape.

# MOSS HEART

Equally as decorative on the door as in the
stairwell, your guests will feel the warmth even
before they enter.

**You will need:**

- Iron wreath
- Moss
- Juniper twig
- Wire
- Pincers

**THIS IS WHAT YOU DO:**

- Squeeze the moss onto the iron wreath.
- At the same time, wind the wire around the wreath to
  secure the moss in place.
- Attach a small juniper twig or similar in the middle of the
  heart shape to decorate.

# NATURE STAR

These stars brings back happy memories of walks
in the woods; memories that will keep you warm on
a cold, winter's night.

**You will need:**

- Twigs
- Hemp rope
- Wire
- Plywood bird (from Panduro Hobby)
- Knife

**THIS IS WHAT YOU DO:**

- Cut the twigs to the same length with a knife.
- Put three twigs together to form a triangle.
- Tie the twigs together at the ends with hemp rope.
- Repeat so that you have two triangles.
- Lay one triangle on top of the other to form a star.
- Tie them together with wire.

# Cut and Glue

When the entire family sits down around the table to prepare for Christmas, you can feel an air of anticipation. I love spending exciting nights enjoying indulgent Christmas food and whispering about all the secret surprises waiting. One of our traditions is gathering the family together for challenges with scissors and paper, or needles and thread. These challenges are very important in determining who gets the nut in the Christmas porridge and who has to sing a Christmas carol by himself on top of a chair!

Evenly cut the foot so the tree can also stand on its own.

# PAPER CHRISTMAS TREE

A simple white paper tree is a classic; elegant both as an ornament on the tree or a decoration on the table. Try making it in different colours, patterns, and sizes to create a crazy Christmas party! The tree shown above is made out of white corrugated card.

**THIS IS WHAT YOU DO:**
- Sketch your own tree either freehand or using the template provided (see Templates).
- Cut out two identical trees.
- Cut the first one from top down, about three quarters of the height of the paper.
- Cut the second one from bottom up, about three quarters of the height of the paper.
- Thread the two pieces together.
- Make a small hole in the top for hanging.

# NANA'S APPLE CIDER

It's not Christmas until we've tasted Nana's apple cider (see photo on Cut and Glue opener).

**You will need:**
- 1 bottle of apple juice
- 1 part blackcurrant juice
- 1 cinnamon stick
- 3 cloves
- 1 small piece of fresh ginger
- Some sugar
- A slice of orange for serving

**THIS IS WHAT YOU DO:**
- Mix all the ingredients together in a pot.
- Heat until it reaches the boiling point.
- Remove the pot from the heat and let it stand for one hour.
- Mix with sugar if desired.
- Heat up to the boiling point before serving.
- Add some orange slices and serve with almonds and raisins.

# WOVEN HEART

This is a simplified version of the traditional woven paper heart. You can use white pieces of paper (or maybe you have some with a traditional Christmas message), a newspaper, or even an exciting fairy tale. There are many possibilities and you can make it as personal as you wish.

## THIS IS WHAT YOU DO:

- Cut out the heart using the template provided (see Templates).
- Weave together one blank piece of paper and one piece with your chosen message.
- Use paper glue at the ends to prevent the pieces from slipping apart.
- Make a hole, thread a string, and create a loop for hanging.

The beautiful woven heart is just as decorative on the Christmas tree, as they are on some branches or with candles.

# CHRISTMAS PORRIDGE

Every Christmas worker needs their porridge.

## You will need:

- 40ml (1½fl oz) water
- ½ tsp salt
- 1 tbsp butter
- 25g (1oz) rice
- 1 piece of cinnamon stick
- 90ml (3¼fl oz) whole milk
- 14g (1 tbsp) sugar

## THIS IS WHAT YOU DO:

- Bring the water to the boil with salt, butter and a piece of cinnamon stick.
- Add the rice and let it boil under a lid until soft (about 10 minutes).
- Dilute with the milk and bring to the boil.
- Let it simmer until it has a nice consistency (about 30–45 minutes).
- Season to taste with sugar and serve with sugar, cinnamon, and a lump of butter in the middle.

# PAPER BALLS

Have fun with a variety of different coloured and patterned papers to create these paper balls. They are just as pretty if you choose a traditional pattern or if you experiment with a funky new design.

## THIS IS WHAT YOU DO:

- Cut 4 paper strips measuring 26 x 2cm (10½ x ¾in).
- Place the strips on top of each other.
- Make a hole in the middle of each strip, as well as 5mm (¼in) in from each end.
- Thread a paper clasp through the middle hole.
- Fold the strips into a circle and thread a paperclip through where the ends meet.
- Separate the strips to make a ball shape.
- Tie a thread around one of the paperclips and make a loop for hanging.

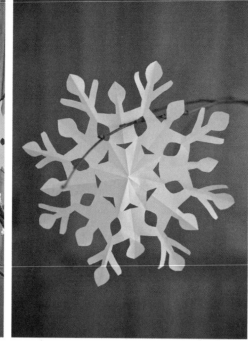

The more cloves you add, the longer the orange will stay fresh. Place them in different patterns and hang with pretty red ribbon.

# HAZEL LEAF WREATH

Hazel leaves have a pretty and elegant form. Recreating the leaf shape with decorative papers in similar shades creates a stylish effect for the wreath.

**THIS IS WHAT YOU DO:**
- Find a hazel leaf to use as a pattern, or use the template provided (see Templates).
- Cut out in decorative paper in similar shades.
- Wind a wreath of wire; making sure it is stable.
- Glue together the paper pieces in a circle, about the same size as the wreath.
- The leaf wreath is attached to the wire using masking tape.

# ORANGE WITH CLOVES

Oranges decorated with cloves in different patterns or with beautiful carvings are a classic tradition and the introduction to Christmas for many.

In France they say that the cloves symbolize the gemstones that covered the three king's presents to Jesus. Cloves also contain ingredients that act as a preservative for the orange.

# HYACINTH HATS

These are essential if you want hyacinths for Christmas. The inspiration for hyacinth hats comes from both Santa Claus and his elves.

**THIS IS WHAT YOU DO:**
- Sketch the cone shape, or use the template provided (see Templates).
- Cut out the shapes from thick paper or thin cardboard.
- Glue along the edges.
- Roll to make a cone and stick in place.
- Make a rosette from the lace of a cake paper.
- Sew a button onto the rosette.
- Sew the rosette onto the hyacinth hat.

# PAPER SNOWFLAKES

These decorative snowflakes are so simple, look great hanging on branches and the children will absolutely love making them! Simply follow the step-by-step diagram in the Templates section.

# BIRD GARLAND

A modern version of the Christmas garland,
without any cross stitching or bells.

**THIS IS WHAT YOU DO:**
- Draw your own bird, or use the template provided
  (see Templates) and cut out in thick cardboard.
- Make two small cuts in the middle of each bird with
  a scalpel.
- Cut out the ribbon to your desired length.
- Tie a wooden bead in one end and thread the birds
  onto the ribbon from the opposite end.
- Leave some distance between the birds so you'll
  have room for some decorations. We have used
  white buttons.

# PAPER STAR

## You will need:
Four paper strips with the same width. The star's size grows with the width of the strips. 1–1.5cm (⅜–⅝in) gives you small stars that look good on the tree. The length = 20 times the width + 10.

Fold each strip in half along the middle and cut the ends so they are slightly tapered. Number the strips 1–4.

Strip 2 hangs from strip 1.

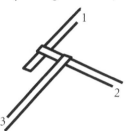

Strip 3 hangs from strip 2.

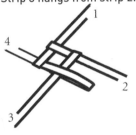

Strip 4 hangs from 3, and the end is pulled through the loop of 1.

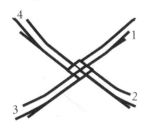

Pull the strips – you have now woven four squares.

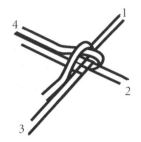

Fold the top part of strip 2 inwards. Fold the top part of 1 in and above 2.

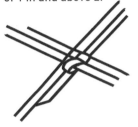

Fold strip 4 inwards above 1. Strip 3 is folded inwards above 4 and under 2 to lock it.

Tighten the strips and put strip 1 to the right.

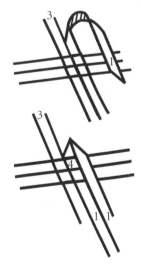

Fold 1 with sharp folds, as shown: first backwards and taper so that it points outwards to the right.

Fold the right part of 1 over the left part and put the end under 4. Repeat this with every other strip until you have four peaks.

Turn the star over and make four new peaks on the other side.

The star will now look like the illustration and look the same on both sides. You will continue with the top strips that we will now call A, B C, and D.

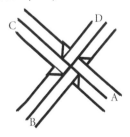

Lift A and pull backwards over C (do not fold, just hold loosely). Make a loop of B and thread the end under where A comes out, so that the end of B comes out in the middle of a flat peak.

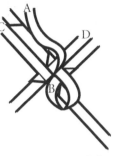

Pull B carefully so it forms a new peak that stands.

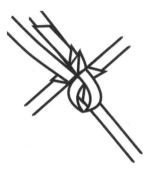

Rotate the star a quarter counter-clockwise and do the same thing with the remaining strips. Rotate and repeat until you have four peaks. Cut the ends of each strip.

# Light and Warmth

In the cold and dark winter season, we seek light and warmth both inside and out. At this time of the year it is actually pretty easy to create small artworks from both wax and ice. Some create a pleasant, warm spirit around the table, while others emphasise the anticipation and excitement of the cold months.

# TERRACOTTA CANDLES

These rustic candle holders are so simple to make, even with the smallest children.

**You will need:**
- 2 terracotta pots
- 2 candles
- Moss
- Candle transfers

**THIS IS WHAT YOU DO:**
- Cut out the transfer you wish to use and put it in a glass of lukewarm water.
- When the transfer comes away from the backing paper, you can place it onto the candle and leave for a few minutes to dry.
- Place the candles in the pots. Fill the pots with stones to hold the candles in place.
- Place moss inside the pots to decorate.

# WALNUT TEALIGHT HOLDER

Filled with walnuts and tied with traditional red ribbon, this lantern is the essence of Christmas.

**You will need:**
- Large glass
- Walnuts
- Linen ribbon
- Tealight candle

**THIS IS WHAT YOU DO:**
- Fill a large glass, well over half, with walnuts.
- Make a pit between the nuts to hold a tealight candle, ensuring the candle is steady.
- Tie linen ribbon around the top of the glass.

# LITTLE LANTERNS

A little nostalgia in all its simplicity.

**You will need:**
- Candle holder
- Cross stitched candle transfer
- Pine branch
- Cotton string

**THIS IS WHAT YOU DO:**
- Cut out your chosen piece of candle transfer and put in a glass of lukewarm water.
- When the transfer comes away from the backing paper, you can place it onto the holder and leave for a few minutes to dry.
- Tie a pine branch to the handle using cotton string.

Snow heart
Maybe a hint to a special friend? Simple, but can mean a lot to the lucky recipient.

Put some sand in the bottom of the lantern so that it will be steady. For safety, you can also put the candle in a glass that can withstand heat.

# PRETTY PAPER LANTERNS

**You will need:**

- Paper lanterns made from flame retardant paper, 16 x 11cm (6¼ x 4¼in).
- Hole punch

**THIS IS WHAT YOU DO:**

- Use a pencil to sketch a figure or an illustration onto the lantern. You can use the snow crystal template provided (see Templates).
- Punch out holes following your sketched pattern.

When you place a tealight candle in the lantern, you've got a decorative advent candle.

# WOOL-WOVEN CANDLE HOLDERS

These are a simple alternative to the crochet candle holders. NB: children might need help using the glue gun.

**You will need:**
- Candle holders or old jars
- Glue gun
- Yarn

**THIS IS WHAT YOU DO:**
- Tie the yarn around the 'neck' of the jar.
- Put glue at even points around the jar while wrapping the yarn close together.
- Finish by making a yarn braid and gluing on top of the jar.

# CROCHET CANDLE HOLDERS

Crochet creates the soft, warm atmosphere that we associate with a white winter.

**You will need:**
- Candle holder
- Crochet needle
- Yarn

**THIS IS WHAT YOU DO:**
- Make the amount of chain stitches you need to fit around the glass.
- Start with 3 chs = 1 double crochet, and continue making double crochets to the end of the row. Each row starts with 3 chs.
- Crochet rows with dcs, 4 rows or what fits your holder. Sew the ends together and thread onto the holder.

On one of the holders we have crocheted a small lace edge on top. Start with 1 sc in the dcs and 2 hds between the dc, 1 sc in the dc. Repeat until the end of the row.

# HANDCRAFTED CHRISTMAS CANDLES

Homemade candles create a special atmosphere. Christmas candles are decorative and pretty, all have personality, and they shed warm light when the sun goes down and they are lit. Older children can help make these candles, while smaller children can watch and learn – maybe next year it will be their turn.

## You will need:

- Premixed wax:1kg (2lb 4oz) is enough for about 20 large candles
- Wicks
- Wooden sticks
- Old pot
- Thermometer
- Potholders
- Scissors
- Wooden spoon for stirring
- Drying rack

The wicks should not come in contact with the water underneath the wax. If this happens, the wicks will attract the water instead of the wax and the candle will 'fizzle' when it burns.

## THIS IS WHAT YOU DO:

- Pour 1kg (2lb 4oz) premixed wax in a large pot.
- Fill with water at a temperature of 70 degrees. (The wax will automatically lay on top of the water.)
- Stir carefully.

Never pour cold water in heated wax, it can spurt and cause burns. For safety, you should keep the lid close by in case of overheating.

- When you start dipping, it's important that the temperature holds 70–75 degrees. IMPORTANT: Use a thermometer and check the heat throughout the session.
- Cut the wicks to the desired length (the same length as the candle).
- Tie the wicks to the sticks.
- Dip the wicks in the heated wax.
- Hold for a little while until the wicks sink and the air bubbles have disappeared then pull up.
- Dip periodically, letting the candles set and cool down between each dip. Use a drying rack or something similar.
- Make sure the candles are hanging.
- Before the last dip: remove the tips at the bottom and make it rounded with your fingertips.
- Hang to dry.

Pull the wicks after the first dips so that the candles turn out straight. Perhaps tie something heavy to the wick. Dip quickly and evenly (10–15 seconds each time). If small tips form under the candle, cut these off.

# THREE KINGS' CANDLES

Create a three-armed candle using the same
steps as the Handcrafted Christmas Candles.

- Cut a wick to the desired length (the length of
  the candle).
- Tie it to the middle of the stick.
- Cut a wick to form the arms.
- Tie each end to the sides of the first
  wick to form a bow.
- Dip once into the heated wax.
- When you pull the wicks out of the wax,
  very quickly attach the bow-shaped wick to
  the wick in the middle by squeezing with your
  fingers.
- Now you've made the foundations of a three-armed
  candle and can continue as described for the
  Handcrafted Christmas Candles.

# DADDY'S SOCKS
Worn is not necessarily the same as worn out!

It is not easy to throw away home knitted socks so we mend them over and over. When dad thinks his socks are through, we give them a new life.

## THIS IS WHAT YOU DO:
- Cut off and use the shaft of the sock. Reverse, making sure the stitches don't come off.
- Sew a seam with a sewing machine by the cut off edge.
- Reverse again. Put a candleholder with a candle inside the new 'candlesock'.

# For the Birds

As soon as the snow falls, it becomes difficult for the birds to find nutritious food. It's time to make a bird feast, or a birds' Christmas party if you prefer, in your backyard or on the porch. Hang the delicious food where you can see it from your window.

# PEANUT WREATH

The wreath is decorative and the bluetit is easily up for the challenge with the shell.

**You will need:**

- Peanuts with shell
- Dried cranberries
- Wire
- Pincers

**THIS IS WHAT YOU DO:**

- Cut the wire to the desired length.
- Thread on a peanut.
- Thread on a cranberry.
- Repeat until the wire is full.
- Tie the ends of the wire.

# ROBIN'S RED APPLE

You will probably also get company from the thrush when you hang up this sweet and nutritious meal.

**You will need:**

- 2 apples
- 1 cone
- Some string
- Small branch from a pine tree
- Scissors
- Awl

**THIS IS WHAT YOU DO:**

- Make a hole through the apples with an awl.
- Cut the string to the desired length.
- Tie a cone in one end.
- Pull the other end through the apples.
- Tie the branch on top.

41

# KING CONE

This is food of kings for tits and bullfinches.

**You will need:**
- Some large cones
- 200g (7oz) white vegetable fat (shortening)
- 200g (7oz) birdseed mix
- Foil

**THIS IS WHAT YOU DO:**
- Melt the white vegetable fat (shortening) in a pot.
- Mix it with the birdseeds.
- Set to cool.
- Squeeze the mix into the cones.
- Wrap the cones in foil.
- Let them set in the freezer.
- Hang in a tree or put them on a plate.

# FOOD BELL

These rustic treats are especially designed for the small birds.

**You will need:**
- A small flowerpot
- Birdseed mix
- White vegetable fat (shortening)
- Rope
- A thin twig
- Some fir branches
- Drill
- Scissors
- Pot

**THIS IS WHAT YOU DO:**
- Drill a hole through the flowerpot.
- Cut the rope to the desired length and pull through the hole.
- Melt the white vegetable fat (shortening) in a pot.
- Mix equal parts of white vegetable fat (shortening) and birdseed mix.
- Pour the mix in the flowerpot.
- Set to cool.
- Tie a twig to the end under the bell.
- Tie some fir branches to the top of the bell.

# THREE-COURSE MEAL

This triple ball hanger provides enough food for everyone in your garden.

**You will need:**
- Foil
- Birdseed mix
- White vegetable fat (shortening)
- Pot
- Scissors
- Thin rope

**THIS IS WHAT YOU DO:**
- Melt the white vegetable fat (shortening) in a pot.
- Mix equal parts of white vegetable fat (shortening) and birdseed mix.
- Set to cool until the mass becomes a little firmer.
- Form a round cup in your hand from the foil.
- Pour the mix in the foil cup and shape into a ball.
- Set to cool.
- Cut some rope.
- When the mix is frozen, remove the foil.
- Wind the rope a few times around the ball.
- Tie multiple balls together and hang.

# BIRD CAKE

You can also welcome the birds with some colourful decorations.

**You will need:**
- A small flan dish
- Birdseed mix
- White vegetable fat (shortening)
- Twig with berries from holly or rowan
- Rope
- Fir branch twig
- Scissors
- Pot

**THIS IS WHAT YOU DO:**
- Melt the white vegetable fat (shortening) in a pot.
- Mix equal parts of melted white vegetable fat (shortening) and birdseed mix.
- Pour the mix into a flan dish.
- Cut the rope to the desired length.
- Stick the rope into the mix before it sets.
- Set to cool.
- Tie the berries to the top of the fir branch.
- Take the 'bird cake' out of the dish when it has set.
- Tie it to the fir branch, underneath the berries.

# CHRISTMAS SHEAF

Christmas sheaf or bird sheaf? The birds love it no matter what we call it!

**You will need:**
- A sheaf of wheat
- 2–3 twigs of fir branch
- A decorative ribbon
- Scissors

**THIS IS WHAT YOU DO:**
- Put the fir branch around the sheaf.
- Cut the ribbon to the desired length.
- Wind the ribbon around the sheaf and twigs two or three times and tie a bow.

If you remove the fir branch twigs and hang the sheaf a few metres (yards) from the house the birds might even be accompanied by some deer.

# CUTE MAKE-UP BAG

Large or small? I bet you know someone deserving.

**You will need:**

- Needle no. 6
- 3-Ply yarn
- Crochet needle no 2.5
- 2 beads
- Wool detergent

**THIS IS WHAT YOU DO:**

- Cast on 40 stitches on needle no. 6.
- Distribute the stitches among 4 needles.
- Knit until it forms a 13cm (5in) square.
- Bind (cast) off the stitches on one side.
- Continue with every other needle K and P on the remaining stitches. The 20 for the flap is half the height of the bag.
- Bind (cast) off and stitch up the bag at the bottom.
- Use a crochet needle to pull a long yarn string through the lip so that you have 2 strings at the end.
- Tie a knot with the two strings.
- Crochet scs with a crochet needle on both strings to a 35cm (14in) length.
- Felt in the washing machine on 60 degrees with wool detergent.
- Let it dry.
- Thread beads on the crochet string to decorate.

# BUSINESS CARD HOLDER

Even in the digital world we need something softer to hold on to.

**You will need:**

- Needle no. 6
- 3-Ply yarn
- Crochet needle no. 2.5

**THIS IS WHAT YOU DO:**

- Cast on 24 stitches on needle no. 6.
- Distribute the stitches among 4 needles.
- Knit back and forth to an 8cm (3¼in) length.
- Switch to red yarn and knit 2 rows.
- Switch back and continue to a 14cm (5½in) length. Bind (cast) off.
- Stitch up the bottom.
- Crochet a red loop on one side of the opening.
- Pull some yarn through to the other side.
- Crochet a large enough ball to lock the holder in the loop.

# WARMING WRISTLETS

Very practical for those with a touch screen on their Smartphones.

**You will need:**

- 3-Ply yarn
- Needle no. 6
- Needle and thread
- Wool detergent

**THIS IS WHAT YOU DO:**

- Cast on 36 stitches on needle no. 6.
- Distribute the stitches among 4 needles.
- Make an edge 1 K and 1 P to a 14cm (5½in) length.
- Continue knitting to an 8cm (3¼in) length.
- Then alternate 2 K and 2 P for 3.5cm (1⅜in) length.
- Bind (cast) off and secure the yarn.
- Put the felt in the washing machine on 60 degrees with wool detergent.
- Let them dry.
- Cut open the holes for the thumbs.
- Secure the holes by stitching along the edges.

# For Little Hands

Children love Christmas! Excitement builds up throughout December with a mix of anticipation, happy memories and pleasant nights. December is filled with evenings around the kitchen table with the children making personal gifts for mummy and daddy, little brother, and good friends. The smallest children might have mixed feelings about Santa and his big bag of toys. The memories from previous years can be powerful.

# FABRIC OWL

A quirky figure that will put the children in a cheerful mood.

**You will need:**

- A suitable piece of fabric
- Cotton
- Needle and thread
- Buttons
- Red crochet lace

**THIS IS WHAT YOU DO:**

- Draw a funny figure on a thick piece of paper, or use the template provided (see Templates) and cut out.
- Place the paper figure on top of the fabric and cut out two equal figures.
- Sew around the edges, right sides together, leaving a reverse opening.
- Stuff with cotton.
- Stitch up the reverse opening.
- Attach different sized buttons for the eyes and nose.
- Embroider a mouth.
- Finish up by tying lace around the waist.

# COLOURFUL GARLAND

This imaginative garland can hang on the Christmas tree, on the hallway mirror, or on a twig in the window. Be as creative as you like!

**You will need:**

- Patterned paper
- Baking cases
- Cotton string
- Scissors
- Glue gun
- Mix of sequins (from Panduro)

**THIS IS WHAT YOU DO:**

- Cut a cotton string to the desired length.
- Make a loop for hanging.
- Cut out different shapes using the template provided (see Templates).
- Glue two sets of the same figures together with the string in the middle.
- Tie on a sequin.
- Make a hole in a baking case and thread it onto the string.
- Continue to the end of the string.
- Finish with a sequin.

# GINGERBREAD HANGER

You don't have to eat them! For many, gingerbread is simply the aroma of Christmas.

**You will need:**

- 150g (5½oz) dairy butter
- 160g (5¾oz) sugar
- 145g (5¼oz) syrup
- 100ml (3½fl oz) cream
- ½ tsp cloves
- ½ tsp ginger
- ½ tsp pepper
- 2 tsp cinnamon
- 1 tsp baking soda
- 450g (1lb) flour
- Cookie cutters
- Cotton thread
- Silver edible balls

**Frosting:**

- 55g (2oz) icing (confectioners') sugar
- 1 egg white
- A few drops of lemon juice

**THIS IS WHAT YOU DO:**

- Mix the butter, sugar, and syrup in a pot.
- Heat on moderate heat until it is all melted. Stir once in a while.
- Leave the batter to cool.
- Mix in the cream while stirring.
- Sift the spices and the baking soda.
- Sift the flour.
- Stir to form a smooth dough.
- Let the dough rest in the refrigerator overnight.
- Sprinkle some flour on your table and knead the dough.
- Roll out in different parts, each being about 3mm (⅛in) thick.
- Cut out stars and hearts with cookie cutters.
- Make a hole in each cookie for hanging.
- Bake at 175 degrees/Gas mark 4 for about 10 minutes, until the cookies are golden.
- Cool off on a grid.
- Decorate with frosting and silver edible balls.

# VIBRANT SHAPES

Christmas doesn't have to be only red and white. New colours create new excitement over old traditions.

**You will need:**

- Colourful patterned paper
- Buttons
- Cotton thread
- Scissors
- Needle and thread
- Glue gun

**THIS IS WHAT YOU DO:**

- Cut out the figures (see Templates) from colourful patterned paper.
- Glue figures of different sizes on top of each other.
- Stitch on some colourful buttons.
- Make holes in the top of the figures.
- Hang with red cotton thread.

Glycerin is a completely safe liquid that thickens water so that glitter can 'flow' within it. You can buy glycerin at the pharmacy.

# SANTA'S SNOWSTORM

This will bring a smile to anybody's face, no matter what age they are.

**You will need:**

- Cleaned jar with a twist off top
- Waterproof glue
- Glycerin
- Glitter
- A small Santa Claus figure
- Water

**THIS IS WHAT YOU DO:**

- Glue Santa's feet to the inside of the lid using waterproof glue.
- Let the glue dry.
- Mix 1 part glycerin with 2 parts of water.
- Add glitter.
- Close the lid with the Santa Claus inside.
- Shake the jar.

# RUDOLPH FOR DADDY

This is how daddy would have looked if he were a reindeer.

**You will need:**

- Canvas on a frame (from Panduro)
- Pencil
- Brush
- Water-based acrylic paint
- Wadding (batting) ball
- Glue gun

**THIS IS WHAT YOU DO:**

- Draw a reindeer head (or another animal) on the canvas.
- Choose a colour that you associate with dad.
- Paint the figure with a paintbrush.
- Let it dry.
- Paint a cheerful contrasting background colour.
- Paint the wadding (batting) ball red.
- Glue the wadding (batting) ball to Rudolph's nose.

# LITTLE SNOWMAN

A funny little man who will give lots of joy to many.

**You will need:**

- White yarn
- Felt
- Glue
- Scissors

**THIS IS WHAT YOU DO:**

- Wind the yard around your hand 10–15 times.
- Form a ball shape.
- Continue to wind around the ball in different directions.
- Repeat to make the ball in two different sizes.
- Glue the two balls to each other.
- Cut out the eyes, nose and scarf from felt.
- Glue on the eyes and nose and tie the scarf around the snowman's neck.

# WOVEN PAPER BRACELET

These bracelets are so pretty, you won't want to give them away!

**You will need:**

- Concentration and patience
- Thin paper (e.g. from a magazine)
- Scissors

**THIS IS WHAT YOU DO:**

- Cut out a strip measuring 10.5 x 3cm (4⅛ x 1¼in).
- Fold long ways so it becomes 10.5 x 1.5cm (4⅛ x ⅝in).
- Fold one more time so the strip becomes 10.5 x 0.75cm (41/8 x ¼in).
- Fold the ends to the middle to make the strip 5.75 x 0.75cm (21/8 x ¼in).
- Fold the middle to close it and to form a V.
- Repeat to make 22 of these figures, using different colours if desired.
- Weave the paper figures together.

# BRAIDED YARN BRACELET

Some colour combinations are great for girls, others are perfect for boys.

**You will need:**
- Yarn in different colours

**THIS IS WHAT YOU DO:**
- Cut strings in three different colours to a suitable length.
- Braid the strings to make a bracelet.
- Tie the ends.

# DECORATED MATCHBOXES

These will be perfect by Grandma's fireplace.

**You will need:**
- Matchboxes
- Felt in different colours
- Cotton
- Glue

**THIS IS WHAT YOU DO:**
- Cut out red felt patches to the size of the matchbox.
- Glue them to the box.
- Cut out the eyes, nose, and mouth from different coloured felt.
- Glue to the box.
- Use cotton as a beard for Mr. Claus and hair for Mrs. Claus.

# WOVEN FLOWER

A special and personal Christmas flower for a colourful relative or friend.

**You will need:**
- Circular loom
- Leftover yarn
- Needle
- Ribbon

**THIS IS WHAT YOU DO:**
- Set strings of yarn in the loom.
- Weave in the middle with a needle, over and under the set strings.
- Pull the yarn tightly towards the middle.
- When the desired size is reached, cut the yarn and tie the ends.
- Fill the 'pillow' with cotton.
- Make two equal circles in different colour combinations.
- Hand stitch them to the 'pillow'.
- Now you've got yourself a flower.
- Tie some ribbon to it for hanging.

# GINGERBREAD GARLAND

When you are making gingerbread (see Gingerbread Hanger), cut out some letters. Make holes with a stick before baking. Let them cool down when finished. Thread ribbon through the holes to make the garland.

# FLOWER HATS

It is wonderful to see something grow in this dark season.

**You will need:**

- Patterned paper
- Scissors
- Glue
- Punch pliers
- Crochet needle
- Cotton yarn

**THIS IS WHAT YOU DO:**

– Cut out the 'hats' using the template provided (see Templates).
– Glue along the edges.
– Roll to make a cone shape and glue. Hold in place until dry.
– Make holes around the opening with the punch pliers.
– Crochet a lace edge with cotton yarn.
– Begin with one sc one round around the hat.
– Then 5 tr in one stitch and 3 sc.
– Repeat until the end of the row.

# CHRISTMAS TREES ON STICKS

Fun and colourful as cake decorations or in a flowerpot in the window.

**You will need:**
- Patterned paper
- Scissors
- Glue
- Ice lolly sticks

**THIS IS WHAT YOU DO:**
- Cut out trees in pairs using the template provided (see Templates).
- Put glue on the back of one tree.
- Place an ice lolly stick on top.
- Close the tree together with the other part.
- Squeeze and hold until dry.

# Almost Christmas

The 23rd December is what they call Christmas Eve Eve, and the living room is filled with beautiful Christmas music. This day is almost as exciting as Christmas Eve itself; you can feel the anticipation as the Christmas tree is brought in, ready to be decorated. This is also a sign that it is almost time for the presents to appear from hiding – it's finally time for guessing and a careful squeeze. Did Santa Claus get my list? What are mum and dad smiling about?

Welcome
Guests are welcomed with a glass of white mulled wine and a slice of exotic pepper cake.

# WHITE MULLED WINE

**You will need (to make 8–10 glasses):**

- 1 bottle dry white wine
- 250ml (9fl oz) water
- 80g (2⅞oz) sugar
- 8 whole cloves
- 2 whole star anise
- 2 cinnamon sticks
- 2 strips of orange peel (preferably from an organically-grown orange)

**THIS IS WHAT YOU DO:**

- Bring the water, sugar and spices to the boil.
- Let it boil on low for 10–15 minutes.
- Put it somewhere cold for 24 hours.
- Add white wine.
- Heat up carefully (the mulled wine should not boil). Strain.
- Pour into the glass and decorate with some spices or raisins.

69

# NAPKIN RINGS

These are so simple and the finishing touch of a small 'Christmas tree' adds to their charm.

**You will need:**
- Crochet thread
- Crochet needle
- Needle and some red thread

**THIS IS WHAT YOU DO:**
- Crochet 21 chs.
- Crochet 7 rows of scs. Start every row with 1 ch = 1 sc.
- Place the ends together and stitch up to make a ring.
- Embroider around the napkin ring with long red stitches.

# GLASS LANTERNS

Charmingly simple and very personal.

**You will need:**
- Kitchen glass
- Kitchen cloths
- Red cotton thread
- Scissors
- Needle
- Heart-shaped buttons (optional)

**THIS IS WHAT YOU DO:**
- Measure the height and circumference of the glass.
- Cut the kitchen cloths to this size, allowing for some room for overlap.
- Wrap the cloths around the glass.
- Stitch up the ends with heart-shaped buttons, cross stitching, or small stitches.

# PLACE CARDS

A red tassel is a constant reminder of who is coming to visit after dinner.

**You will need:**
- Red yarn
- Glue/glue gun
- Cards
- Cotton thread

**THIS IS WHAT YOU DO:**
- Wind some yarn around your hand a few times.
- Cut it off and use the end to tie up the middle of the roll you've made.
- Cut the ends and fold at the middle.
- Wind the yarn around a few times at the top and tie.
- The tassel is attached to the card with cotton thread.

# WINTER WARMER HOT CHOCOLATE

**You will need:**
- 100 ml (3½fl oz) water
- 600 ml (21fl oz) whole milk
- 1 dark chocolate bar
- 1 cinnamon stick

**THIS IS WHAT YOU DO:**
- Boil the water in a pot.
- Cut the chocolate into pieces and put into the water to melt.
- Add the milk and cinnamon stick.
- Heat carefully to the boiling point.
- Pour into mugs.
- Put milk foam on top (using a steamer).
- Use a cinnamon stick as a stirrer.

# HEARTFELT HANGERS

These wool felt decorations give a warm, Christmas feeling.

**You will need:**

- 1 thick sheet of paper
- Wool felt
- Wool felt string
- Scissors
- Needle and cotton thread

**THIS IS WHAT YOU DO:**

- Trace the heart shape (see Templates) onto a thick piece of paper and cut out.
- Pin the heart to the wool felt.
- Cut out felt hearts.
- Sew around the edge of the heart with white cotton thread.
- Make a loop from wool felt string for hanging and stitch it onto the back of the heart.

# CHRISTMAS TREE PILLOWS

It is unbelievable what you can create from a used teatowel.

**You will need:**

- Teatowel
- Scissors
- Cotton thread
- Needle and thread

**THIS IS WHAT YOU DO:**

- Find two nice segments of the teatowel.
- Draw a 14cm (5½in) square and cut out.
- Place them right sides together, attach a loop of cotton thread and stitch up.
- Leave a small hole for reversing and stuff the pillows.

# BEAUTIFUL ANGEL

Equally pretty on the Christmas tree and as an egg warmer.

**You will need:**

- Wool felt
- Red felt
- Wool felt thread
- Scissors
- Needle and cotton thread

**THIS IS WHAT YOU DO:**

- Trace the angel and star shape (see Templates) onto thick paper and cut out.
- Pin the paper angel to the white wool felt.
- Cut out 2 angels from the white wool felt.
- Pin the paper star to the red felt and cut out.
- Stitch the star to the angel with white cotton thread.
- Buttonhole stitch the two wool felt angels together.
- Leave an opening at the bottom.
- Make a loop from wool felt thread and sew it to the back of the angel.

# BEADED CHRISTMAS TREE

A natural and Nordic look that fits in with the wool felt theme.

## You will need:

- Beads, 5cm (2in) in diameter (from Panduro)
- Beads, 2.5cm (1in) in diameter
- Beads, 1.5cm (⅝in) in diameter
- Leather string

### THIS IS WHAT YOU DO:

– Make a tie at the end of the string.
– Thread the largest bead.
– Thread the middle-sized bead.
– Thread the smallest bead.
– Make a loop at the end of the string and tie.

# KNITTED HEARTS

Give dad's old socks a new life.

## You will need:

- Dad's old knitted socks
- Scissors
- Sewing machine
- Yarn
- Wadding (batting)
- A button

### THIS IS WHAT YOU DO:

– Cut out two of the same heart shape from the socks. Be careful so the stitches don't run.
– Place the two hearts right sides together.
– Sew almost the whole way around with a sewing machine, leaving an opening so you can reverse it.
– Fill with wadding (batting).
– Stitch up the hole.
– Make a braid from the yarn.
– Make a knot in each end to create tassels.
– Make a loop from the braided yarn.
– Attach it to the heart with a white button.

# YARN BAUBLES

The children are easily engaged, and the spirit around the table will probably bring the adults some childhood memories.

## You will need:

- Leftover yarn

### THIS IS WHAT YOU DO:

– Wind the yarn around your hand 10–15 times and make a small ball.
– Continue to wind the yarn around the ball in different directions.
– Finish by tying the ends around the top layers.
– Make a loop.

# WOOL FELT SOCK CALENDAR

Wool felt is a traditional feature in Norwegian homes but not usually in the form of a calendar.

**You will need:**

- Wool felt
- Yarn
- Scissors
- Punch pliers
- Cernit clay (White Fimo soft modelling clay)
- Print letters and numbers

**THIS IS WHAT YOU DO:**

- **To make the socks**, cut out the sock shape using the template provided (see Templates).
- Put two socks together.
- Stitch up around the edges using buttonhole stitches.
- Make holes along the top edge with the punch pliers.
- Crochet a lace edge in the holes, making 2 double crochets in each hole.
- Attach a small bell and the numbered star (see below).

- **To make the numbered stars in cernit clay (White Fimo soft modelling clay)**, roll out the clay into a thin wafer on a plastic surface.
- Use a cookie cutter and cut out 24 stars.
- Print the numbers into the clay.
- Make a hole in the stars with a stick.
- Put the stars on a baking sheet with parchment paper.
- Heat the oven to 100 degrees/Gas mark ¼.
- Let the stars dry on the oven for 15–30 minutes.
- Take the stars out and leave to cool.

# FAMILY ADVENT CALENDAR

There will be excitement around the table when the lucky one gets to open the surprise of the day from the rest of the family. The little sister can start with December 1st, on December 2nd it's the little brother's turn...

**You will need:**

- 12 white bags
- 12 striped bags (you can buy the bags from large craft stores)
- 1 small daily calendar
- Patterned tape
- Blu-tack

**THIS IS WHAT YOU DO:**

- Decide the order in which your family members will receive their surprises.
- Place the gifts in the bags and fold the top to close them.
- Pull out December 1–24 from the daily calendar.
- Secure the tops with patterned tape while at the same time attaching the number from the calendar.
- Use Blu-tack to attach the bags to the wall. Place the bags in the shape of a tree.
- This tree also deserves a star on top.

# SOCK CALENDAR TREE

Christmas starts early with this tree. In addition to the calendar, the child will also have 12 new pairs of socks.

**You will need:**

- 12 pairs of socks with different designs
- 24 neutral buttons, 3cm (1¼in) in diameter
- Number decorations
- Ribbon
- 24 surprises
- Some branches from a tree

**THIS IS WHAT YOU DO:**

- Glue numbers 1–24 onto the buttons.
- Attach one button to each sock.
- Leave a surprise in each sock.
- Close the sock with ribbon.
- Hang the socks on the 'early Christmas tree'

80

# 24 LITTLE ONES

A classic setting, almost like a collage. The little wrapped treasures will fill you with a fuzzy feeling inside every day.

**You will need:**

- Canvas on a wooden frame (from Panduro)
- Grey, white and black labels (from Panduro)
- Black, white, grey and red cardboard
- Clasps
- White wrapping paper
- Red and white cotton thread
- Scissors

**THIS IS WHAT YOU DO:**
- Draw the numbers 0–9 on cardboard (see Templates). Use these numbers as a template when you cut out numbers in different colours. Make numbers from 1–24.
- Glue the numbers to the labels.
- Measure, equally space and secure the labels.
- Insert the clasp through the hole in the label and through the canvas.
- Split the legs of the clasp so the label is attached to the canvas.
- Wrap 24 small surprises.
- Tie red and white thread around the presents.
- Hang them around the head of the clasp.

# CALENDAR FULL OF WISHES

What do you wish for in the time before Christmas? To gather the whole family for a night of baking? A night at the theatre? That dad does the Christmas cleaning? There are many options, you just have to be creative.

**You will need:**
- Some thick paper with different patterns
- Number stickers
- Clasps
- Cotton thread
- Punch pliers
- Mobile with 24 clips
- Scissors

**THIS IS WHAT YOU DO:**
- Trace the shapes (see Templates) onto the paper and cut out.
- Attach the number stickers 1–24 to the cut out shapes.
- Make a hole in the middle using punch pliers.
- Cut out a paper strip and write your wish.
- Make holes in each end of the paper strip.
- Insert the clasp through the figure and the paper wish in the back.
- Split the legs of the clasp to secure your wish.
- Make a hole in the top with punch pliers.
- Thread cotton through the hole and hang in one of the clasps of the mobile.

# ADVENT CANDLELIGHT

Candlelight makes an intimate Christmas atmosphere.

**You will need:**

- 4 candle holders
- 4 candles
- Wool felt
- Wood buttons
- Scissors
- Needle and thread

**THIS IS WHAT YOU DO:**

- Cut out felt in a rectangular shape corresponding to the shape of the holder. Include some overlap.
- Embroider the text and numbers using backstitch.
- Stitch up the ends with a button.
- Thread over the holder.

# CHRISTMAS OF THE HOBBY CARPENTER

A plank is all you need. Not to mention someone that can use the jigsaw.

**You will need:**

- A plank
- A jigsaw
- A drill
- Décor paint
- Paintbrush
- 4 candle holders made of metal
- 4 small candles

**THIS IS WHAT YOU DO:**

- Draw the letters on a thick plank.
- Cut out with a jigsaw.
- Cut the letters flat on the bottom so they can stand up straight.
- Drill holes on top of the letters for the candle holders.
- Paint the letters white and let them dry.
- Install the candle holders on the top of the letters.
- Draw the numbers from the templates provided (see Templates).
- Paint the numbers with décor paint and let it dry.
- Place the candles.

# NORDIC CANDLES

Simple, elegant, natural...

**You will need:**

- Jar
- Decorative sand
- Candles
- Number transfers
- Larch twig with cones
- String
- Twine
- Scissors

**THIS IS WHAT YOU DO:**

- Fill a jar to over half full with decorative sand.
- Decorate the candles with numbers from 1–4 with transfers made for candles.
- Put the candles all the way down to the bottom of the jar, so they stand up straight.
- Carefully bend a larch twig with cones around the jar.
- Tie up the ends with twine.

# CHILDREN'S ADVENT CANDLES

The children need to be able to help prepare for Christmas too.

**You will need:**

- Tin
- Walnuts
- 4 candles
- Blu-tack

**THIS IS WHAT YOU DO:**

- Use Blu-tack underneath the candles.
- Push the candles down to the bottom of the tin. Make sure they stand up straight.
- Fill with walnuts.
- Simple as that!

# Christmas Flowers

Christmas flowers are a symphony of beautiful shapes and colours; some with their elegant crowns, others with their majestic elegance. The Christmas spirit just isn't there without some homemade flower arrangements to welcome your family and friends.

# HOLLY

It has been said that the name of the tree originates from the crown of thorns worn by Christ, which was made from holly. There is also a lot of superstition attached to holly. It is supposed to have many qualities, such as protecting from accidents, evil, and ghosts. Good to know at this dark time of year.

Holly is the only hardwood tree in Norway that keeps its leaves and stays green thought the whole winter. The tree requires some heat and in Norway, you can find it along the coast from Kragerø to Smøla. It is also unique in a different way; you can almost never find the male and female flower on the same tree. The fruit, or berries, are bright red and very decorative. But watch out, they are poisonous for humans if eaten and can cause sickness and vomiting – a little reminder if you have small children.

# HOLLY WINTER BERRIES

This kind of holly, that has the name *Ilex Verticillata*, also has a name that is tied to the native Americans. In the earlier days they used the berries for medical treatment and called it Fever Berry. *Ilex Verticillata* is a bush found in the wetlands of eastern Canada and the United States. In the winter it will shed its leaves and the berries will be left as big, red temptations for the small birds all through the cold season. I guess we can say that Fever Berries are still making themselves useful. Back in Norway, all we can do is be excited about the fresh colour and energy it gives us throughout the winter.

# COTTON VASE

A tip for someone that wants a new life for an old vase; try a decorative wrapping in a typical Nordic design.

**You will need:**

- Cotton yarn or wool
- Needles or circular needle, depending on the yarn

**THIS IS WHAT YOU DO:**

- Cast on stitches depending on the size of your vase.
- Knit and purl every other time to the end of the needle.
- On the next row, do purl and knit. Continue until it measures the height of the vase.
- Stitch up the ends.
- Thread over the vase. The vase is now as good as new!

# AMARYLLIS

A myth tells us that amaryllis can survive fire, water, and drought. This is most likely just a good story, but what is definitely true is that the bulb is tough and has an extraordinary will to grow. You can make an amaryllis bloom even without putting the bulb in soil. Give it a couple of weeks and you'll get a strong stem that will bloom into an impressively beautiful flower.

Amaryllis has a tall and leafless stem with large star shaped flowers on top. It can grow to be 70cm (28in) tall and the flowers can grow to 10cm (4in) in diameter. The colour of the flowers range from shades of white to pink and red. For a beautiful amaryllis, put the bulb in a vase but make sure that only the roots are in water. If it gets too much water, both the roots and the bulb will die. Change the water 2–3 times a week. Leave the vase somewhere warm (20 degrees) for 4–6 weeks. As soon as you see buds on the bulb, move it to where it has the most light.

# AMARYLLIS IN A JAR

Take the flower out of the plastic pot and put green moss around the potting soil. Place the amaryllis in a glass jar. Tie ribbon around the jar and attach some decorations – we chose a heart made from a birch log.

# BULBS IN A TUB

It can be decorative to put some amaryllis on a plate or in a tub so you can see the beautiful bulb structure. Remember to cleanse the roots with water on a regular basis.

# AMARYLLIS ARRANGEMENT

An arrangement of amaryllis is always a decorative element. Put some moss on top of the potting soil to give the arrangement a softer look. Be very careful with water.

# CHRISTMAS ROSE

There is something soft and sensual about the Christmas rose and some say that it is the most beautiful Christmas flower. The Christmas rose can be left outside until there is frost on the ground. When you take the flower inside, leave it in a cold place and it will last longer. Put some moss on top of the potting soil and use some cones to embellish.

# MOSS STAR

A star-shaped zinc pot forms the framework of this forest floor of hyacinth, reindeer moss, cones, and some fragrant cinnamon sticks.

# ANEMONE

The anemone has an interesting line of relatives. You can find the anemone on every continent, with the exception of Antarctica, and it is in total related to about 150 different species.

The origin is unknown but the flower is more than likely from the eastern parts of the Mediterranean and the Middle East. The Greek God Adonis was supposedly killed from the tusks of a wild boar during hunting. When Aphrodite sprinkled nectar over Adonis' body, his blood turned into a red Anemone. Others claim that Anemone is from the Greek word for wind; 'anemos'. Maybe this explains why it has spread to every corner of the world.

Despite its widespread nature, the Anemone is not very hardy or lasting. If you put it in direct sunlight it will bloom quickly and wither just as fast. They are beautiful but very delicate; similar to other delicate things.

When you buy a bouquet of Anemones you have to remember to slit the stems before you put them in cold water. In cold water they will grow slowly and you can enjoy your bouquet for up to one week. The water should be changed daily. The flower needs light, but try to avoid direct sunlight and draft.

The Anemone needs a little extra attention and care.

## ANEMONES IN THE WINDOW
Sharp colours and haughty lines are like a Christmas fairy tale against the white snow outside. Put anemones, larch twigs, hyacinth and pine branches in different glass vases for a transparent arrangement.

# POINSETTIA

Rumour has it that this delicate flower was originally smuggled out of Mexico during the 19th century by the American ambassador and hobby botanist, Joel R. Poinsett. Other stories take it back 2000 years to the stories around the crucifixion of Jesus. The reason why the poinsettia is one of our most beloved Christmas flowers probably has to do with the fact that it blooms in December – right in the middle of the cold and dark season.

The poinsettia is very delicate and should not be left in draft or be given much water. With light, heat, half-dry soil, and good care, the poinsettia can bloom from November to January. The red 'leaves' are not really the flower – in the middle of the red leaves you can find some small yellow flowers. In the summer, the whole plant stays green. If you want the top leaves to be red, put the plant in a dark room for at least 12 hours a day for a few weeks.

# CHRISTMAS BEGONIA

The Christmas begonia is the result of a successful crossing made from France in 1891. We can safely say that it is perfect for the Nordic winter. The Christmas begonia likes short days and long nights, and it blooms only during the winter.

The Christmas begonia favours a low inside temperature, about 18–20 degrees. Avoid drying up the soil; it likes continuous moisture and lukewarm water. Many people use slightly hard water.

Avoid cold drafts directly on the flower. Despite liking short days, it won't dislike it if you place it where it gets lots of daylight (no direct sunlight). Daylight is especially important when the flower is developing its buds.

# MINI POINSETTIA

The mini poinsettias give a beautiful and soft expression when the soil is covered with moss. Attach the moss with winding wire. Now, the mini poinsettias will look great on the table, in a wood bowl or a rustic plate. If you feel even more creative, you can tie a string around the stem all the way down by the moss, and hang the mini poinsettia in the Christmas tree.

# MOSS POT

Wind some wire around the moss to keep it in place. Continue with red/white string so the moss is shaped like a pot around the soil. Attach a metallic label with a Christmas greeting. Put the begonia in a rustic bowl and wrap it in cellophane. The greeting is now a little more exciting.

# FELT FLOWER POT

Decorated felt cachepots are very pleasing to the eye. This one is decorated with flowers but here you have many options of using the shapes and colours of Christmas.

**You will need:**

- Flat felt
- Red and white cotton fabric
- Needle and thread

**THIS IS WHAT YOU DO:**

- Cut out the two shapes in felt.
- Stitch up the short sides of the rectangular shape using blanket stitches.
- Pin up the round shape so it forms into a pot.
- Stitch up the two shapes using blanket stitches.

# FABRIC FLOWERS

**THIS IS WHAT YOU DO:**

- Draw a circle on the fabric of your choice, about 9.5cm (3¾in) in diameter.
- Fold in about 2mm (¹⁄₁₆in) and tack (baste) stitch around the circle.
- Tighten with the tacking (basting) thread and attach in the middle of the flower.
- Attach the flower to the pot.

# HYACINTH

Place the hyacinth in sandy soil in September/October. Only about two thirds of the bulbs should be covered in soil. Hyacinth are easy to care for and don't need much water. When it sprouts you can take it out of the soil and wash the roots carefully in water. Now you can make fragrant decorations with glasses, pots and bowls.

Don't place the hyacinth bulbs in water, but let the roots access the water available. When blooming it is important that the roots get plenty of water. To make the blooms last longer, place the hyacinth in a cold place overnight.

Slit hyacinth should not be in deep water, only about 2–3cm (1¾–2¼in) up the stem. This is an important rule to remember for all slit bulb flowers.

# FLORISTS' SECRETS

Cold water holds a temperature of about 10 degrees. Lukewarm water holds 20–25 degrees. Warm water holds about 50 degrees and above.

**THIS IS WHAT YOU DO:**
- Tulips like it best in cold water.
- Roses like warm water.
- As a general rule, flowers that have a soft stem prefer cold water.
- Slit flowers and other flowers with a hard stem prefer warm water.
- The water temperature is important for the flower to quickly begin its water absorption.
- When you buy cut flowers make sure that they put the stems in wet paper or something similar.
- Drying of the stem can happen in as little as 15–20 minutes.
- Slit the stems at an angle so that they get a large surface for absorption.
- Use a clean knife. Even fat from your skin can clog the delicate pores.
- Don't use scissors; it will make the pores flat.
- Remove leaves from the water. The leaves bring bacteria that will clog the pores.
- Flowers need clean water every day.
- If you use preservative in the water, you only have to change it once a week.

**HOW TO MAKE YOUR OWN PRESERVATIVE:**
- 1 litre (1¾ pints) of water
- 10ml (2 tsp) vinegar
- 25g (1oz) sugar

- Stir the mixture until the sugar is dissolved

Don't place cut flowers in direct sunlight or by heaters. Keep the flowers in a cold place overnight so that they last longer.

# TULIPS

At the end of the 16th century the tulip came to the Netherlands from Turkey. A misunderstanding made the name. A famous Flemish author was trying to describe the shape of the flower by comparing it to a turban, or dulband in Turkish. The people of the Netherlands then thought that this was the name of the flower. Even though the misunderstanding was too difficult to correct, the tulip gained interest nationally.

A Persian legend tells about a young man that loved a woman so much it killed him. The love was too much for the heart to bear and it burst with drops of blood falling to the ground. On this exact spot it started growing tulips, which grew into a tulip meadow. The tulip is our most popular cut flower and the colours all have different meanings: red is for love, white for purity, orange for heat.

As a cut flower, the tulip has a short life expectancy of 8–10 days if you treat it nicely. Make sure the stems are wrapped in wet paper when you buy them. Cut the stems straight off with a sharp knife/ scalpel and place the flowers in ice-cold water as high as a quarter of the way up the stem. Don't add any preservative in the water and keep topping up with water so that the level is constant. Don't place tulips in direct sunlight and place them somewhere cold overnight.

# HYACINTH

In the literary myth, Hyacinth was a beautiful boy loved by the God Apollo. Hyacinth died very young in dramatic circumstances and the God Apollo then made him into a flower. According to the myth, the petals of the flower were coloured by the tears from the God Apollo. The myth aside, the flower is beautiful and colourful, with the aroma of Christmas.

# Tasty Presents

Christmas brings excitement and joy; particularly the joy of surprising your friends with a holiday treat featuring the best of your tasty festive favourites.

# JOHAN'S ANISE AND FENNEL SCHNAPPS

This present is ready in five minutes – before you leave for the Christmas party. The lucky receiver can then follow the development of the schnapps for the following week.

**You will need:**

- 2 large tsp aniseed
- 2 large tsp fennel seeds
- 2 large tsp dried juniper
- 350ml (12fl oz) clean spirits, or 60%
- A suitable bottle

**THIS IS WHAT YOU DO:**

- Crush the seeds and the juniper in a mortar.
- Pour the mix into a clean bottle.
- Add the spirits.
- Seal it with a cap.
- Let it stand for 5–7 days.
- Filter the schnapps.
- Clean the bottle and pour the schnapps back.

**The schnapps is now ready for tasting.**

Adjust the label to fit the bottle or use the template provided (see Templates) as a basis. Decorate the label with the name of the product or with a Christmas greeting. Punch holes in both ends and tie around the bottle with Christmas string or ribbon.

# MUSTARD AND HORSERADISH HERRING

Mustard herring is a classic on the Scandinavian Christmas table. This one has an almost creamy texture with a touch of horseradish. Mmm...

## You will need:

- 400g (14oz) herring
- 100ml (3½fl oz) mayonnaise
- 50ml (2fl oz) crème fraiche
- 2 tsp sweet mustard
- 2 large tsp Dijon mustard
- 1 small tbsp sugar
- 1 tbsp white wine vinegar
- 3 tsp finely grated horseradish
- Pepper
- Chives
- Jar

## THIS IS WHAT YOU DO:

- Rinse the herring well in a strainer. If they are not watered out you should place them in cold water for about one hour.
- Cut the herring into pieces of about 1.5cm (⅝in).
- Place them in a jar.
- Mix all the ingredients and season with pepper.
- Pour the sauce over the herring and mix well.
- Finely chop the chives and place on top.

# CHRISTMAS MUSTARD

With this recipe you get a wonderfully spicy, half sweet and tasty mustard.

## You will need:

- 100ml (3½fl oz) red wine vinegar
- 100ml (3½fl oz) vinegar, 7%
- 100g (3½oz) yellow mustard seeds
- 75g (2¾oz) brown mustard seeds
- 160g (53/4oz) sugar
- 2–3 ground cloves
- Salt
- Jar

## THIS IS WHAT YOU DO:

- Mix the vinegar with the red wine vinegar.
- Add the seeds and let it swell for 2 days.
- Mix half of the mass in a blender until smooth.
- Pour the remaining seeds and the mass into a casserole dish and add sugar.
- Heat on low, carefully stirring for 10–15 minutes until the sugar has melted.
- Season with ground cloves and salt.
- Pour into a clean jar and place it in the refrigerator.

# FIGS IN BRANDY

An exclusive and tasteful present that goes perfectly with soft Italian vanilla ice cream.

**You will need:**

- 8 fresh figs
- 500ml water
- 240g (8½oz) sugar
- 1 cinnamon stick
- Grated orange peel from one orange
- 200ml (7fl oz) brandy
- Jar

### THIS IS WHAT YOU DO:

- Boil water, cinnamon, sugar, and orange peel on low heat under a lid for about 15 minutes.
- Remove the pot from the heat.
- Use a strainer to remove the orange peel and cinnamon stick.
- Add brandy.
- Rinse the figs in flowing water.
- Use a toothpick to make 10–15 holes in the figs.
- Place the figs in a clean jar.
- Pour over the brandy pickle until it completely covers all the figs.
- Let the mix cool off at room temperature before you put the lid on.
- Store in the refrigerator.

# CHRISTMAS VINEGAR

This vinegar both tastes and smells like Christmas. Even the look of it will give you Christmas spirit.

**You will need:**

- 2 cinnamon sticks
- 1 finger joint size of fresh ginger
- 1 orange (preferably organic)
- 3 star anise
- 1 bottle white wine vinegar
- 1 suitable gift bottle

### THIS IS WHAT YOU DO:

- Clean the bottle, rinse with vinegar and place it in the oven at 120 degrees/Gas mark ½ for about 20 minutes.
- Cool off at room temperature.
- Clean the orange in flowing warm water.
- Cut the orange peel into different shapes.
- Cut the ginger into small pieces.
- Place it in the bottle with the cinnamon sticks and the star anise.
- Pour on the white wine vinegar.
- Put on the top and let it stand for a few days.

# TASTY OIL

In-between all the large family dinners at Christmas, we should also make room for some lighter seafood. This oil is perfect for both grilled lobster and fresh shrimp.

**You will need:**
- 2 sprigs of thyme
- 2 small tbsp of dried chilli flakes
- 500ml (16fl oz) olive oil
- 1 suitable gift bottle

**THIS IS WHAT YOU DO:**
**Important:** Clean the bottle, rinse with vinegar and place it in the oven on 120 degrees/Gas mark ½ for about 20 minutes. Cool off at room temperature. The bottle must be completely dry on the inside. The smallest drop of water can be enough to spoil the oil.

- Pour the chilli flakes into the bottle.
- Add the sprigs of thyme.
- Fill the bottle with the olive oil.
- Put on the top and let it stand for a few days.

# PICKLED CLEMENTINES

Clementines pickled in sugar, vanilla, cinnamon, star anise and cloves make the ultimate taste of Christmas. They are perfect with vanilla ice cream and grated dark chocolate.

**You will need:**
- 10 clementines
- 1 vanilla pod
- 3 cinnamon sticks
- 5 star anise
- 5 cloves
- 1kg (2lb 4oz) sugar
- 1 litre (1¾ pints) water
- Jar

**THIS IS WHAT YOU DO:**
- Mix the sugar and water in a pot with the seeds of the vanilla pod and the cinnamon sticks. Add star anise and cloves.
- Boil for about 15 minutes.
- Peel the clementines and place them in a jar.
- Pour the pickle into the jar until it covers all the clementines.
- Put on the lid and leave to cool.

Place the salted almonds in a bowl and wrap in cellophane. Make a small label (see Templates), with some cardboard or thick paper. Decorate it with a drawing or a friendly Christmas greeting. Make a hole through the label and tie it to a small wooden spoon for a lovely present.

Pour the tasty Christmas muesli mix into a suitable paper bag. Fold the top into a tip and make a hole to put a red ribbon through. Bind around the bag and tie a label to it with a nice breakfast greeting.

# CHRISTMAS MUESLI

Christmas muesli is a joy to make, yet an even greater joy to give away. It is so tasty, it is almost like almost like eating candy for breakfast. Make a large portion while you're at it so you have some for family and friends, young and old.

**You will need (to make 20 portions):**
- 150g (5½oz) dried figs
- 150g (5½oz) nut mix (walnuts and hazelnuts)
- 200g (7oz) rolled oats
- 250g (9oz) seed mix with the same amounts of wheat, barley, rye, and oat
- 100g (3½oz) raisins
- 100g (3½oz) dried cranberries
- 1 heaped tsp cinnamon
- ½ tsp salt
- 100ml (3½fl oz) honey
- 100g (3½oz) coconut

**THIS IS WHAT YOU DO:**
- Preheat the oven to 175 degrees/Gas mark 4.
- Put baking paper in the bottom of a deep roasting tin.
- Finely chop the figs.
- Finely chop the nuts.
- Mix all the ingredients and spread it all out on the roasting tin.
- Sprinkle with cinnamon and salt.
- Pour honey over the mix.
- Place the roasting tin in the oven to dry for about 30 minutes.
- Stir periodically.
- Play close attention so the muesli doesn't burn.
- Towards the end you can add the raisins and cranberries.
- Leave to cool.

Now you've made a sweet and tasteful Christmas greeting for 20 of your closest family and friends.

# SALTED ALMONDS

Served heated on cold, winter nights.

**You will need:**
- 200g (7oz) almonds
- 3 tbsp salt
- 200ml (7fl oz) water
- 10g (¼oz) butter

**THIS IS WHAT YOU DO:**
- Bring the water to a boil.
- Dissolve the salt in the boiling water.
- Add the almonds.
- Cover with a lid and let the almonds soak for 15 minutes.
- Strain the almonds.
- Cover a baking tray with baking paper.
- Spread the butter and the almonds around the tray.
- Roast in the middle of the oven on 150 degrees/Gas mark 2 for 20 minutes.
- After the butter has melted, turn over the almonds a couple of times.

# CHRISTMAS SALT

Christmas salt is an easy-to-make, colourful and decorative present, bursting with flavour.

**You will need:**

- 250g (9oz) sea salt
- 1 large tbsp pink peppercorns
- 1 tsp dried chilli flakes
- 1 clean bowl, bottle or jar.

**THIS IS WHAT YOU DO:**

– Mix the salt and the spices.
– Pour into the jar.

For a thoughtful gift, thread some ribbon through the hole in the crispbread and tie together. Decorate with a pine branch and a small Christmas greeting then wrap the crispbread in cellophane.

# CRUNCHY CRISPBREAD

A crunchy element for your Christmas breakfast, seasoned with your favourite festive spices.

**You will need:**

- 500ml (18fl oz) lukewarm water
- 50g (1¾oz) yeast
- 2 tsp salt
- 2 tbsp oil
- 1 tbsp anise spice
- 1 tbsp fennel seeds
- 420g (14¾oz) coarse rye flour

**THIS IS WHAT YOU DO:**

- Crumble the yeast in the bowl of the mixer.
- Add lukewarm water.
- Run the mixer carefully so that the yeast dissolves.
- Add salt, oil, anise, fennel and rye flour.
- Run the mixer until the dough is soft and smooth (5–7 minutes).
- Place a towel over the bowl and let the dough rise for at least 1 hour.
- Preheat the oven to 250 degrees/Gas mark 9.
- Sprinkle flour onto baking paper.
- Roll out the dough and cut it into about 15 bun-shaped pieces.
- Push the buns together, cover with clingfilm (plastic wrap) and let them rise for another 20 minutes.
- Roll out the buns onto thin sheets.
- Use a plate or something similar as a template and cut out rounded shapes.
- Use a small glass and cut out a hole in the middle.
- Place the round sheets on a baking tin covered with baking paper.
- Make small holes with a fork.
- Bake for 5–7 minutes.

If the crispbreads need more drying time, you can put them in the oven at 75 degrees for 20–30 minutes with the door partially open. Preferably use the convection setting on your oven.

# CHOCOLATE-COVERED APRICOTS

If you end up with some leftover chocolate, simply make some extra candy.

**You will need:**

- Dried apricots
- Amaretto (Italian liqueur)
- Good quality dark chocolate

**THIS IS WHAT YOU DO:**

- Leave the apricots to soak in Amaretto for about an hour.
- Move the apricots onto paper towel so the Amaretto can dry.
- Melt the chocolate using a double boiler.
- Dip the apricots into the melted chocolate.
- Place the apricots on a sheet of baking paper until the chocolate dries.
- Serve immediately.

# Sweet Christmas

Start your day by buying decorations, sugar spheres, frosting, chocolate, cream, truffles, coconut and everything yummy to make all the sweet temptations of Christmas. It's not possible to picture a Christmas without marzipan either – it would be like a Christmas without a Christmas tree. Good luck, and remember: you're allowed to be tempted during the Christmas preparations!

# MARZIPAN MR. AND MRS. CLAUS

These will be the children's favourites.

**You will need:**

- White figure marzipan (from Odense)
- Red marzipan
- Sticks
- Cake decorations

**THIS IS WHAT YOU DO:**

- Roll small balls from the white marzipan.
- Stick a large and a small ball together on a stick.
- Make hats, braids, and scarves from red marzipan.
- Roll a thin snake from white marzipan for the arms and the edges of the hats.
- Add cake decorations for the eyes, nose, mouth, buttons, etc.

112

# ROASTED ALMONDS

A real treat for friends and family.

**You will need:**

- 120g (4½oz) almonds
- 200ml (7fl oz) water
- 160g (5¾oz) sugar

**THIS IS WHAT YOU DO:**

- Mix the almonds, sugar and water in a frying pan.
- Let it boil until you can see the sugar starting to brown, foam frothing, and the mass starting to thicken.
- Remove the frying pan from the hot stove and stir so that the sugar coats the almonds.
- Continue boiling until the sugar is brown.
- Pour the almonds onto some baking paper.
- Separate the almonds before you leave them to cool.
- Store in an airtight jar at room temperature.

# MARZIPAN HEARTS

An Italian poet so appropriately once said: 'a good heart will quickly learn the language of love'.

**YOU WILL NEED:**

- Homemade marzipan
- Rolling pin
- Icing (Confectioners') sugar
- Cookie cutters in 2 different sizes
- Dark chocolate
- Cake decorations

**THIS IS WHAT YOU DO:**

- Roll out the desired amount of marzipan.
- Sprinkle icing (Confectioners') sugar onto it.
- Cut out one large and one small heart with the cookie cutters.
- Put the small heart on top of the large heart.
- Melt some dark chocolate in a double boiler.
- Decorate each heart with a drop of chocolate and add cake decorations as desired.

114

# WALNUT CHOC MARZIPAN BALLS

Big temptations for small occasions.
Or was it the other way around?

**You will need:**
- Homemade marzipan
- Walnuts
- Good quality dark chocolate

**THIS IS WHAT YOU DO:**
- Roll out small balls of marzipan.
- Press a walnut down onto every ball.
- Melt the dark chocolate in a
  double boiler.
- Decorate the marzipan balls with thin
  stripes of chocolate.

115

# CRANBERRY AND PISTACHIO MARZIPAN BALLS

Delicious, rich, and covered in dark chocolate.

**You will need:**

- 200g (7oz) homemade marzipan
- 10g (¼oz) dried cranberries
- 10g (¼oz) pistachio nuts
- 1 tsp Amaretto (Italian liquor)
- Dark chocolate
- White chocolate

**THIS IS WHAT YOU DO:**

- Cut the marzipan into small cubes.
- Run the marzipan, cranberries, pistachios and liquor in a blender.
- Knead into a soft mass.
- Roll out balls to your desired size.
- Melt the dark chocolate in a double boiler.
- Dip the marzipan balls in the chocolate.
- Place them on baking paper.
- Sprinkle some white chocolate on top.
- Leave to cool and store in a cool place.

# CHOCOLATE TRUFFLES

You may call it a symphony of sweet tasting experiences.

**You will need:**

- 300g (10½oz) good quality dark chocolate
- 20g (¾oz) butter
- 3 tbsp cream
- 2 tsp brandy
- Grated orange peel

**THIS IS WHAT YOU DO:**

- Melt the chocolate and butter in a double boiler.
- Leave to cool a little.
- Stir while you add cream, brandy and grated orange peel.
- Mix well and leave to cool. This will make the chocolate easier to work with when you roll it into balls.
- Roll the balls in coconut, pistachio or cocoa.
- Store in a cool place.

# FLORAL NOUGAT CASES

Nougat is made from hazelnut – you can recognize the flavour.

**You will need:**

- 200g (7oz) nougat
- 100g (3½oz) walnuts
- Candied flowers

**THIS IS WHAT YOU DO:**
- Melt the nougat in a double boiler.
- Chop the walnuts and mix with the nougat.
- Pour the nougat into small baking cups. You can use a spoon.
- Decorate with a candied flower.
- Place the confectionary somewhere cold for about 1 hour.
- Store in a cool place.

# CHOCOLATE ROUNDS

Good confectionary can be really easy to make.

**You will need:**
- 200g (7oz) good quality chocolate
- Hard candy mints

**THIS IS WHAT YOU DO:**
- Cut the chocolate into pieces and melt in a double boiler.
- Cover a baking tin in baking paper.
- Use a spoon and drip rounds out of chocolate onto the baking paper.
- Chop the hard candy mints into pieces.
- Put small pieces of hard candy mints onto each chocolate round.
- Place in the refrigerator for the chocolate to set.

119

# Wrapped with Love

Wrapping symbolizes the excitement and anticipation whilst the presents are sat under the tree. The atmosphere is electric whilst waiting for everyone to finish their Christmas dinner so the unwrapping can begin, with or without Santa Claus. A personal wrapping can be just as exciting as the present itself – it can show both love and care. The templates for all the figures used in this chapter are at the back of the book.

1.

2.

3.

# RED AND WHITE CHRISTMAS

Red is the traditional Christmas colour in the Nordic countries. Red gnomes, red candles, and red tablecloths are things that we all associate with Christmas. Red is also the colour of love, which goes hand-in-hand with the message of Christmas. White is the colour of joy, light and purity. The combination of red and white is therefore perfect for Christmas.

**THIS IS WHAT YOU DO:**

1. The white wrapping paper is embellished with a red stamp of hearts made of cross stitches.
- The rosette is made from white cake paper, attached to a small red rosette (from Panduro).

2. Wrap the box with white linen fabric. Lock with decorative masking tape (Washi-tape).
- Tie a red ribbon with white polka dots around the present.
- On the white label we've attached a handmade rosette made from fabric (see Fabric Flowers).
- The bottom present is wrapped in white wrapping paper.
- Attach the ribbon with decorative masking tape (Washi-tape).

3. A stack of beautiful presents in red and white. Use plain or striped string, knitted belts, or belts made from corrugated cardboard. There are many options and they all have the essence of Christmas.

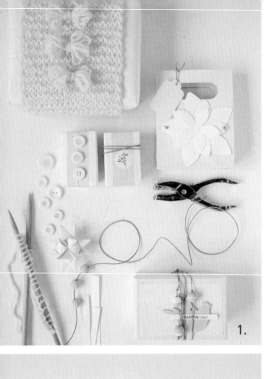

1.

2.

3.

5.

GLEDELIG JUL

## White Christmas

4.

6.

124

7.

TIL LILLE BROR

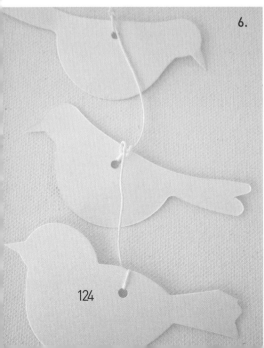

8.

# WHITE CHRISTMAS

White is the colour of joy, light and purity. A white Christmas can symbolize many different things depending on what Christmas means to you. It therefore feels right to place white in a historical, Christmas perspective. You will find templates for all the figures used in this chapter in the back of the book (see Templates).

**THIS IS WHAT YOU DO:**

1. White on white. There any many shades of white and you can also mix them.
- Wrap the box in white wrapping paper. Knit a belt from white yarn.
- Make some bows from the same yarn.

Large and small white boxes can be decorated with buttons, punched figures, stars and decorative masking tape (Washi-tape), amongst other things. If you want to create a contrast, you can use brown leather cord.

2. Wrap the box in white wrapping paper and make a belt from white linen.
- Whirl a leather cord a few times around the present.
- Finish by making a paper star and attaching it to the leather cord (see Templates).

3. Use a white box and decorate it with a white belt, made from paper.
- Wrap some thick string around the box.
- Thread some buttons on a string and attach them, scattered randomly around the box.
- Finish by tying the string around the box.

4. Choose wrapping paper in varying shades of white for the different boxes.
- This will create a calm and elegant present.

5. Cut out a piece of decorative paper a little smaller than the lid of the box.
- Glue the paper to the lid.
- Attach the bird on top with glue.
- Make a paper strip and write a Christmas greeting on it.
- Glue the strip as a belt across the bird.
- Paint a few beads and thread on a leather cord.
- Wrap the leather cord around the present.

6. Wrap a box in white wrapping paper.
- Choose some patterned or textured paper.
- Here we've used pre-made punched figures (you can find these at paper/craft stores.) You can also use the birds shape provided (see Templates).
- Use a hole punch and tie string between the birds, then attach them to the present.

7. Cut out paper strips from newspapers, magazines etc. measuring 1.5 x 18cm (⅝ x 7in).
Fold the strips in half and make a hole at one end.
- Place all the strips on top of each other and lock it using a clasp.
- Lock in the back and spread the 'arms' to make a rosette.
- Write a message or use as a nametag.

8. Buy a white paper bag.
- Trace the flowers (see Templates).
- Transfer to decorative paper and cut out one in each size.
- Make a hole in the middle and attach the flowers together with a clasp.
- Make holes in two of the leaves and attach the flower to the bag by making holes in the bag and tying leather cord on both sides.
- Trace and cut out a label (see Templates) that you can attach to the handle with leather cord.

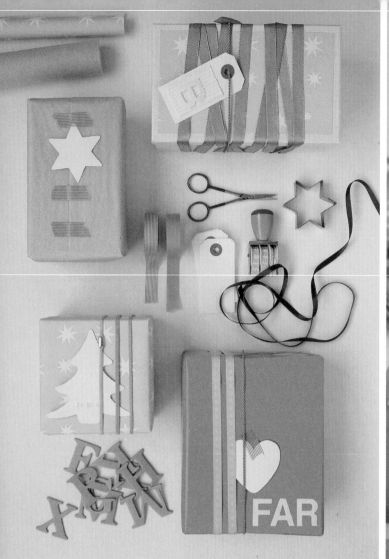

# GREEN CHRISTMAS

A green Christmas can mean many things. Many probably want the meaning to be focused around a better climate and environment. Let's start with some green, environmentally friendly wrapping paper.

### THIS IS WHAT YOU DO:

1. Wrap the box in glossy paper. Cut out stars, trees, hearts and other shapes from thick, white matt paper and use to decorate the boxes.
- Use stickers instead of traditional labels.
- Add different types of ribbon for a finishing touch.
- Make belts from corrugated cardboard or ribbon and tie neon coloured bells to the ends.

2. Fresh green colours and white stars. The tree label is made from environmentally friendly paper and is given a date stamp – perhaps for the expiration of its content?
- Hair ties can be used as ribbons around the presents.
- Add beads or braids for a touch of sparkle.

3. A box within a box adds a level of intrigue and excitement and makes the perfect present for a special friend. Use a small box for a 'large' present.
- Wrap the small box with a big ribbon.
- Place it in a clear, acrylic box (Plexi-box) and tie ribbon around it.

# A NEUTRAL CHRISTMAS

Recycled, real and all natural; there is something really honest about neutral-coloured products. With some warmth and imagination, the brown tones will rise and look proud. Boxes can be made from different materials: sometimes you will need a really hard box and other times a plywood box may be the natural choice. Add some brown decorated masking tape (Washi-tape) and a heart made out of birch bark and the work is done.

The belt on the middle present is made from an old teatowel. The name is simply cut out from recycled cardboard and tied to the top.

The box at the top of the pyramid is decorated with pages cut out of an old book.
- The rosette on the top is also made from book pages (see step 7, White Christmas)

Paper bags are a great alternative and simple to use as wrapping.
- Fold over the top and make a hole.
- Thread a string.
- Thread a button or a bead on each side to use a lock.
- Decorate the bag with punched crystals or labels with paper letters.

We tend to use square and rectangular boxes when wrapping presents, however tubes made of cardboard or paperboard can offer a fun and practical alternative.
- Cut down the tube to desired length and put the lid back on.
- Use sticker letters and numbers (perhaps for the name of the receiver).
- Staple a paper rosette to the top.

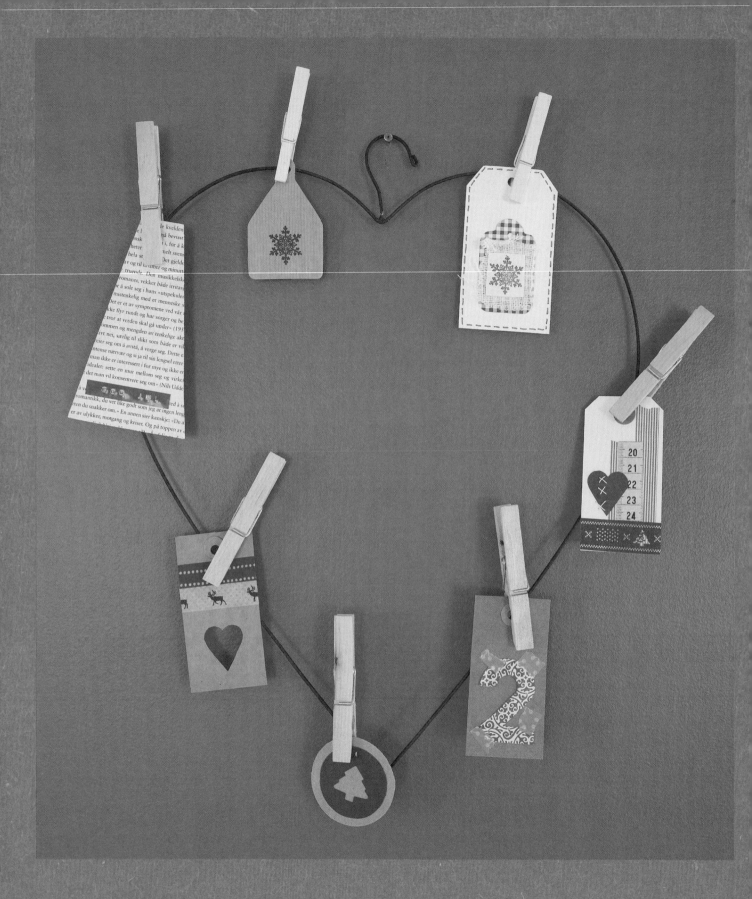

Homemade labels are great for decorating. Get out
your scissors, paper, tape, cardboard, and so on.
Try the ones we've described or design your own.

  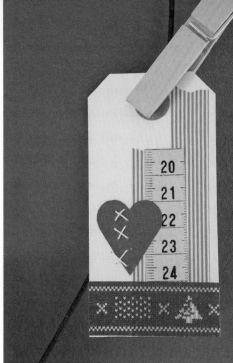

# LAVISH LABELS

### Label 1.
- Cut out a traditional shape from thick white cardboard (use an old dry-cleaning label as a template).
- Make a hole in the top with a hole punch.
- Draw small red stitches along the edge with a red felt pen.
- Cut out a smaller label from red-checked cardboard.
- Glue it to the cardboard.
- Cut out a small piece of linen.
- Glue the fabric to the red-checked cardboard.
- Stick a red snowflake to some white cardboard and cut out.
- Finish by attaching the last piece of cardboard to the linen.

### Label 2.
- Use the template provided (see Templates) and cut out the shape in newspaper and cardboard. Glue the newspaper to the cardboard.
- Write a Christmas greeting with a label writer (Dymo) and attach it to the label.
- Make a hole in the top with a hole punch.

### Label 3.
- Use a pre-made label.
- Use decorative tape in different patterns.
- Cut out a heart from red paper.
- Cross stitch the heart to the label to finish.

## NAME THE DATE

The choice of materials for this simple card come from the root of Nordic design.

## TRENDY X-MAS

Hopefully the recipient will get the hint!

- Take a picture of what you want for Christmas.
- Glue it to a card made from thick, coloured paper.
- Stitch on a button.
- Glue on the letters: X-MAS.

# CHRISTMAS STAR

One of the safest signs that Christmas is coming.

- Use a four-sided card. You may wish to use a card with torn edges (from Panduro).
- Cut out a slightly smaller square from red paper and glue to the front of the card.
- Trace the star (see Templates) onto thick white paper and cut out.
- Attach the star to the card with a clasp.

# TEXTURED SNOWFLAKE

A simple card that gives a warm feeling.

**THIS IS WHAT YOU DO:**
- Choose cardboard in two shades of earth colours.
- Cut out a different-sized square from each colour.
- Glue the smaller square to the larger one.
- Cut out a smaller square from a teatowel and glue onto the card.
- Attach a punched snowflake on top.

# WISE OWL

Say it with your favourite animal or bird.

**THIS IS WHAT YOU DO:**
- Cut out a square from cardboard containing wood.
- Cut out a smaller square from decorative paper.
- Trace the owl (see Template) onto thick white paper and cut out.
- Glue the three pieces together with the owl on top.
- Print a greeting and cut into a small paper strip.
- Glue the strip across the card.

# A MUSICAL GREETING

A thoughtful gift for those who like to sing.

**THIS IS WHAT YOU DO:**
- Record this year's Christmas music to a CD.
- Put the CD in a tracing paper envelope.
- Print out your message on a small paper strip.
- Glue the paper strip to the front of the envelope.
- Make a four-sided card from red cardboard.
- Glue the CD envelope to the inside of the card.

# A JOYFUL MESSAGE

Send this card to one of your loved ones.

**THIS IS WHAT YOU DO:**
- Use a 10 x 15cm (4 x 6in) piece of plywood (from Granit).
- The letters are punched out from cardboard containing wood.
- Tie up the letters with some red elastic
- Tie the elastic at the back.

# CARD À LA TREAT

A fun greeting containing a special recipe for a Christmas treat.

**THIS IS WHAT YOU DO:**
- Cut out two identical cards in corrugated paper.
- Type up your special recipe and print it out on white paper.
- Cut out the recipe in the same shape as the card.
- Glue the recipe onto one of the cards.
- Cut out the heart (see Templates) and glue on to the front.
- Hole punch the top of the cards and tie them together with some coarse linen ribbon.

# INDULGENT ORANGE SLICES

This is a real Christmas treat and a simple way to wrap it.

**THIS IS WHAT YOU DO:**
- Dry the orange slices following the instructions (see Dried Citrus/Apple Slices).
- Melt a quality chocolate bar in a double boiler.
- Dip the dried citrus slices in the hot chocolate.
- Place the slices onto a sheet of baking paper and leave the chocolate to cool.
- Wrap with red velvet ribbon.

# The Scent of Christmas

What is the ultimate scent of Christmas? Fir branches? Hyacinths?
Soap? Incense? Maybe the spices that we use? There are many
spices that we use only at Christmas. You can call them Christmas
spices or the scent of the holidays, warmth and joyful nights.

# APPLE WREATH

**THIS IS WHAT YOU DO:**
- Dry the apple slices following the instructions (see Dried Citrus/Apple Slices).
- Get a few pinecones a couple of days before making the wreath.
- Leave them to dry by the fireplace so they can open into beautiful shapes.
- Start off with a stiff ring or thick wire.
- Attach the cones with wire.
- Tie dried apple slices, cinnamon sticks and juniper twigs to the wreath with red cotton string.
- Make a bow from red linen ribbon.

# APPLE CANDLESTICK

A fun, fruity candlestick that will light up a decorated table.

**THIS IS WHAT YOU DO:**
- Choose an apple that can stand on the table.
- Make a hole in the apple using a seed remover.
- Put a metal candleholder in the hole.
- Place the candle on a plate with dried fruit and Christmas spices.

# APPLE GARLAND

**THIS IS WHAT YOU DO:**
- Dry the apple slices following the instructions (see Dried Citrus/Apple Slices).
- Let the apple slices cool off after taking them out of the oven.
- Make a hole in the middle of each slice.
- Thread a red ribbon through each slice and make a garland. It is just as decorative both on the tree and in the window.

# CINNAMON DÉCOR

Easy-to-make and fragrant, both on the table and on the tree.

**THIS IS WHAT YOU DO:**
- Tie 3–4 cinnamon sticks together with red cotton and make a loop for hanging.
- Finished!

# DRIED FRUIT

It is simple to make these beautiful and fragrant citrus and fruit slices. They are decorative with their colours and shapes and they also taste very good.

# CHRISTMAS POTPOURRI

Or a symphony of cinnamon sticks, bay leaves, dried citrus slices, star anise, and cloves. A nice little present for a pre-Christmas party; Christmas starts when the bag is opened.

**THIS IS WHAT YOU DO:**
- Fill a cellophane bag with spices and dried citrus.
- Close the bag and make a small hole, the right size for a thin ribbon.
- Thread an apple slice on a linen ribbon and tie up.

# Cake Galore

'To bake cakes and set a pleasant table is always nice. Not only when you have guests – a real housewife also enjoys surprising her family with something tasty.' A very appropriate quote from a Swedish book, published in 1962.

Forget all the jokes
you've heard about
the fried cruller.
It is not a cake
for the poor.

# SERENA COOKIES

When Santa Claus is out, the time is right for candles and cookies.

**You will need:**
- 250g (9oz) flour
- 2 tsp baking powder
- 2 tsp vanilla sugar
- 100g (3½oz) sugar
- 150g (5½oz) butter
- 1 egg
- Crystal sugar, egg, and chopped almonds for topping.

**THIS IS WHAT YOU DO:**
- Mix the flour, baking powder and vanilla sugar.
- Crumble the butter into the mix.
- Whisk the egg and add the sugar.
- Knead the dough well.
- Cover with plastic film and let it cool off for at least an hour or overnight.
- Roll the dough into long pieces, cut into slices then roll into balls.
- Place the balls on a tray lined with baking paper.
- Squeeze the balls flat using a fork.
- Brush with egg.
- Sprinkle crystal sugar and chopped almonds on top.
- Bake in the middle of the oven at 175 degrees/Gas mark 4 for 10–12 minutes.

# FRIED CRULLER

Fried crullers are one of Scandinavia's favourites from the seven kinds of cakes we make for Christmas.

**You will need:**
- 4 egg yolks
- 80g (2⅞oz) powdered sugar
- 75ml (2½fl oz) cream
- 2 tbsp brandy
- ½ cardamom
- 200g (7oz) flour

**THIS IS WHAT YOU DO:**
- Whisk the egg yolks and powdered sugar.
- Add the whipped cream and brandy.
- Sift the flour and mix it gently with the cardamom.
- Work as little as possible with the dough so it doesn't become too sticky.
- Cover with clingfilm (plastic film) and leave to cool overnight.
- Roll out the dough a little at the time.
- Cut out oblong, corner tips using a pastry wheel cutter.
- Make a cut in one end and thread the other end through the hole.
- Deep fry until they are light yellow.
- Drain on paper towels.

# KRUMKAKE

Everyone likes krumkake in one form or another. You can serve it with ice cream, berries, whipped cream, or with some chocolate and lemon soufflé – the list goes on and on.

**You will need:**
- 3 eggs
- 150g (5½oz) sugar
- 150g (5½oz) flour
- 150g (5½oz) butter
- ½ tsp cardamom

**THIS IS WHAT YOU DO:**
- Whisk the egg and sugar.
- Add melted, cooled butter.
- Stir in flour and cardamom.
- Cover and let it rise for 1 hour.
- Pour the batter onto the middle of a heated krumkake iron, using one spoon per krumkake.
- Squeeze the iron together.
- Bake until they have a golden colour.
- Make a cone from the cakes before they cool.

# GINGERBREAD

The following quote was once written about a similar cake: 'Suitable for a family with many naughty children. The troubled mother can eat it with butter along with her afternoon coffee.'

**You will need:**

- 500g (1lb 2oz) dark syrup
- 2 tbsp dairy butter
- 250g (9oz) sugar
- 450g (1lb) flour
- 1 egg
- 1 tsp cloves
- 1 tsp cinnamon
- ½ tsp pepper
- 250ml (9fl oz) lukewarm milk
- 1 lemon
- 4 tsp baking powder

**THIS IS WHAT YOU DO:**

- Crush the cloves in a spice grinder.
- Mix the cloves, sugar, flour, cinnamon, pepper and baking powder.
- Heat the syrup to a lukewarm consistency.
- Add the milk and stir.
- Add the juice from the lemon and stir.
- Add melted butter and an egg and stir.
- Add all the liquid ingredients to the flour mix.
- Mix well.
- Pour the batter into a bread tin.
- Bake at the bottom of the oven at 180 degrees/Gas mark 4 for 30–45 minutes.

146